MADE IN GOD'S IMAGE. REALLY?

MADE IN GOD'S IMAGE. REALLY?

GR8 RELATIONSHIPS

EQUIP PRESS

Colorado Springs

MADE IN GOD'S IMAGE. REALLY?

Published by Equip Press, Colorado Springs, CO

First Edition: 2023
Made in God's Image, Really? / (GR8 Relationships)
Paperback ISBN: 978-1-958585-45-0
eBook ISBN: 978-1-958585-46-7

EQUIP PRESS

Colorado Springs

CONTENTS

INTRODUCTION

The book of Genesis states clearly we are all created in the image of God.

God created man in His own image; in the image of God He created him; male and female He created them,

Genesis 1:27, NKJV

The fact that we are created in God's image drives everything about the design of human beings, both men and women. God had a specific objective for creating, and it's interesting to see how that objective plays into His relationship with us. It proves that He is not just a big bad God sitting in Heaven waiting to pounce when we make a mistake. He created us in His image. When we see that He created us to be a reflection of Him, it floods us with light and an understanding of why we are on the planet and what our relationship with Him should be.

So, to understand what all this means, let's start by exploring God's objective with creation.

God's Purpose for Creating

Battles between the camps of Creation and Evolution prompt the question, "Did God create Adam and Eve from nothing, or did man evolve from apes?"

Genesis 1 and 2 are part of that battleground but the importance of the facts in these chapters goes beyond that difference in the origin of man, Creation or Evolution.

> *Then God said, "Let Us make man in Our image, according to Our likeness; let them have dominion over the fish of the sea, over the birds of the air, and over the cattle, over all the earth and over every creeping thing that creeps on the earth. So God created man in His own image; in the image of God He created him; male and female He created them. Then God blessed them, and God said to them, "Be fruitful and multiply; fill the earth and subdue it; have dominion over the fish of the sea, over the birds of the air, and over every living thing that moves on the earth."*

Genesis 1:26-28, NKJV

Anything in God's Word is valuable and important for us and our journey as Christians, but most of us don't think of these verses as the theological foundation of the Bible's message. Most see salvation as the central and most important message in God's Word. In no way am I saying or implying that the incredible gift of salvation is not a critical message of the Bible.

Consider what Dr. Roy Zuck says:

The fundamental question that must be asked of the creation accounts is, "So what?" The judgment that all these (created) things were "good" is of course a statement of purpose. It suggests that creation serves aesthetic ends at least. But aesthetics alone is an insufficient basis on which to build the eternal, divine objective. To see that objective in more concrete and specific terms one must ascertain the particular purposes attached to the creation of man, because it is man who is the image of God and for whom the rest of creation provides a setting.

This leads to Genesis 1:26–28, the first and foundational text to articulate the functional aspect of the creation of man. The formal, anthropological aspect is found in Genesis 2. The first part of the statement of purpose is that man is made in the image and likeness of God (1:26a), a purpose reiterated as having been accomplished with the added nuance of gender distinction (v. 27) ... The text speaks not of what man is like but of what he is to be and do. Just as images or statues represented deities and kings in the ancient Near East...so man as the image of God was created to represent God Himself as the sovereign over all creation.[1]

Roy Zuck

If his thinking is correct, the creation of man and woman is part of the theological center of the Bible and needs to be understood to clarify how they were created and for what.

He further provides a great summary that man is created in the image of God to:

- ... represent God Himself as the sovereign over all creation
- ... reign in a manner that demonstrates his lordship, his domination (by force if necessary) over all creation[2]

Everything was great for man and his relationship with God until Satan entered the picture. Satan's deception of Eve and the ultimate disobedience by both Adam and Eve put the earth under Satan's rule. He is now the ruler of this world. He is the one with dominion as you can see in the two verses in the gospel of John shown below.

Now is the judgment of this world; now the ruler of this world will be cast out.

John 12:31, NKJV

> . . . *of judgment, because the ruler of this world is judged.*

John 16:11, NKJV

Since man's sin ushered Satan in as ruler of the earth, God's plan of salvation through the death and resurrection of Christ ultimately reestablishes mankind as the ruler. So, salvation can be considered as deliverance from one place or state to another. That means salvation takes mankind from the current status of fallen (due to disobedience to God's plan) back to the original plan.

Salvation is an awesome gift from our gracious Father and is the Lord's way of redeeming us from the Fall of Man. God uses salvation to revoke Satan's rule and hand it back to mankind. Looking at salvation through the restorative lens underscores the importance of the book of Genesis and all that we can learn from it.

Though many only see Genesis as an explanation of beginnings, it is vastly more important. It is foundational to understanding the problems for relationships and marriages.

The first three chapters of Genesis describe the following and more:

- Man's creation and design (what he was designed to do)
- Woman's creation and design (what she was designed to do)
- Foundation used for both of those designs
- Importance of and how designs are used

in marriage
- Contract for Godly marriage
- Blueprint for how we sin
- Structure we follow as the path of least resistance to sin
- Problems for marriages when not following God's roles
- God's judgment upon the woman (curse) and its impact on relationships and life
- God's judgment upon the man (curse) and its impact on relationships and life

Genesis is critical to understanding the entirety of God's revelation. It provides the *how* and *why* foundation for understanding the design of men and women, their relationships, and how life works. Throughout the Bible it is important to remember that God demonstrates His purpose to bring mankind back into the original design so man can reign with Him, as He planned from the beginning.

REFLECTIVE QUESTIONS

- How has your perspective changed regarding the fundamental message of the Bible? How do you see the salvation message differently than you did before?

_____

_____

_____

_____

- God created a redeeming plan for mankind after Adam and Eve succumbed to Satan's lies. How does this relate to His love for you?

_____

_____

_____

_____

- From the following list, which topics do you believe will impact your current thinking? What benefit will you receive from learning about these designs?
    - Man's creation and design (what he was designed to do)

- Woman's creation and design (what she was designed to do)
- Foundation used for both of those designs
- Importance of and how designs are used in marriage
- Contract for Godly marriage
- Blueprint for how we sin
- Structure we follow as the path of least resistance to sin
- Problems for marriages when not following God's roles
- God's judgment upon the woman (curse) and its impact on relationships and life
- God's judgment upon the man (curse) and its impact on relationships and life

IMAGE OF GOD –
FOUNDATIONAL AND
PREVALENT

Several scriptures relate to God creating man in His own image and are foundational for ultimately understanding God's design for mankind, specifically for men and women.

Since God provided His Word to change our bad thinking and renew our minds, your study of God's Word helps clarify your thinking on specific issues you face in life. Old Testament prophecy is connected to the New Testament's fulfillment through the appearance of Jesus on the earth and His purpose here. As you study further you see that the truths support each other and are linked together. Finally, after more study, you find the perfection of God. More things are connected than you ever thought!

Oswald Chambers, an early-twentieth-century Scottish Baptist evangelist and teacher who wrote *My Utmost for His Highest*, provides an extremely simple method to experiencing richness in our lives based on what we find in God's Word. He says, *you do not reason your way through God's Word, you simply obey each part that you read, then God reveals more to you.* What Chambers says is reality because God is *perfect*. Starting there gives you more motivation to trust all that He has said in His Word.

Since God is *perfect*, all of His Word works together, supporting and expanding our ability to see, appreciate, and worship Him. Dr. Marlin Howe magnified my belief in our *perfect* God, when he showed from God's Word how God's image is aligned with the designs of men and women.

Understanding the image of God demonstrates why men's and women's designs are uniquely different. It provides insight into how marriage and relationships work best and how the designs fit together. Without the clarity of God's image, you probably will not see how much of life, and especially relationships, depend upon two basic components that can describe the image of God.

So why are men and women designed so differently? We don't need to speculate. God explains all of it in His Word! Mankind is created in His image, and He is reflected in the design of men and women. Additionally, His image extends far beyond the design of men and women.

Predominant View

Many teach about God's Image being comprised of three elements: emotions, intellect, and will. We have emotions and He has emotions. We have intellect and He has intellect. We can choose, have a will and He can choose and has a will. While it is true those are commonalities with our Creator, God's Word does not describe emotions, intellect and will as all the components of His Image.

Below are some statements showing how the image of God is often taught:

> *"Therefore, God has provided the soul of man with intellect, by which he might discern good from evil, just from unjust, and might know what to follow or to shun, reason going before with her lamp . . . To this he has joined will, to which choice belongs."*[3]

John Calvin

> *"There is a long history of debate concerning the nature of the "image of God." In what respect did God make man like Himself? Some have felt the key to likeness was an original holiness . . . So most commentators have agreed that the uniqueness of man is the key to understanding image. We know from the Bible that God has*

emotions, values, chooses, appreciates beauty,
demonstrates creativity, makes distinctions
between right and wrong, loves and even
sacrifices Himself for the sake of others. We know
from the Bible that God is a Person, with identity
and individuality."[4]

Lawrence O. Richards

"Human life was created in (lit., "as," meaning
"in essence as") the image of God (v. 27). This
image was imparted only to humans (2:7).
"Image" is used figuratively here, for God does
not have a human form. Being in God's image
means that humans share, though imperfectly
and finitely, in God's nature, that is, in His
communicable attributes (life, personality, truth,
wisdom, love, holiness, justice), and so have the
capacity for spiritual fellowship with Him."[5]

John F.Walvoord and Roy B. Zuck

These men are excellent theologians who likely
have wrestled with this issue far more than I have. What
they say is true. What is also true, however, is that an
even clearer option is available. If this other option is
accurate, it makes a massive difference in understanding
relationships, marriages, and life.

Another Option

The following is a list of verses using *image of God* or implying the image of God. If you want, please look at each and study them.

> *Then God said, "Let Us make man in our image, in our likeness," …So God created man in his own image, in the image of God He created him; male and female He created them.*

Genesis 1:26, 27, NJKV

> *. . . for in the image of God He made man.*

Genesis 9:6, NKJV

> *. . . (we are) conformed to the image of His son . . .*

Romans 8:29, NKJV

> *. . . (man) reflects the image and glory of God. . .*

1 Corinthians 11:7, NKJV

> *. . . we shall also bear the image of the heavenly*

1 Corinthians 15:49, NKJV

. . . (we are) changed into the same image . . .

2 Corinthians 3:18, NKJV

. . . Christ, who is the image of God . . .

1 Corinthians 4:4, NKJV

. . . (Christ) is the image of the invisible God . . .

Colossians 1:15, NKJV

All those passages are worth your study, but only the two Genesis passages are important for this current discussion. Why? First, the other passages do not speak about the image of God and the creation of males and females. Second, a rule of scriptural interpretation is *the rule of first cause.* It means the first time a word or phrase is used, that is most likely the meaning that God desires to be assigned to that word or phrase. With that in mind, Genesis 1:26-27 is the first time God speaks about His image. And Genesis 1:27 is the only verse to provide more information where it says,

> *So God created man in his own image, in the image of God He created him; male and female He created them.*

Genesis 1: 27, NKJV

Two significant elements show up in the verse: 1) God created man (mankind) in His own image, and 2) male and female were created.

What if those two elements are related? For example, is the "image of God" linked to "male and female?" Please understand me: I am not implying that God is male and female! Is God telling us that He not only created mankind as male and female but somehow displays His Image in the distinct attributes of males and females?

A simple approach would be to examine the design, definition, and behaviors of males and females.

First, Genesis 2 gives words that describe the design and purpose of a "male" and "female."

- Adam – Genesis 2:5, 15 tells us God created Adam to till (work), tend (cultivate, maintain), and keep (watch over, observe, protect). A man is designed to work
- Eve – Genesis 2:18 states God created Eve to be a helper (aid, support), comparable (suitable, appropriate, belong, a fit), so man should not be alone (companion, relate). A woman is designed to relate

Second, English dictionaries define males and females with lists of adjectives.

- Male – masculine, manly, macho, virile, manlike; not – feminine, girlie, effeminate, womanish
- Female – womanly, feminine, lady, effeminate (mostly as derogatory of men)

Finally, medical research provides adjectives and behaviors for the hormones in males and females.

- Testosterone – brawn, strength, power, muscular, aggressive, assertive, separate, dominant, disconnected, alone
- Estrogen-progesterone – emotional, moody, sensitive, approachable, attractive (physically and relationally)

So, summarizing the words from the Bible, dictionaries, and medical research, you could have the following:

- Male = powerful, separate (supports the "work" design)
- Female = relational, belong (supports the "relational" design)

Therefore, is it reasonable to describe the image of God as "powerful and relational" or "separate and belonging?"

I realize this is not in-depth research, but using those summary words to describe males and females seems rather obvious and intuitive. Even so, here is one last critical element. Christian scholars and theologians often use two words to describe God: transcendent and immanent. Statements such as,

> *"One God . . . above all, and through all, and in all"*

Ephesians 4:6, NKJV

indicate that God stands in a relationship of both transcendence and immanence to the created order. In that he is *"above all"* and *"over all" (Romans 9:5)*. He is the transcendent God, and independent of his creation, self-existent and self-sufficient. On the other hand, in that He is *"through all, and in all,"* He is immanent in His creation (though distinct from it), and creation is entirely dependent on his power for its continued existence.

> *In Him all things hold together*

Colossians 1:17, NKJV

and

> *. . . in Him we live and move and have our being.[6]*

Acts 17:28, NKJV

Note transcendence says God is *"above all"* and *"over all."* The definition of transcendent contains words like "apart from, surpassing, incomparable, and preeminent." On the other hand, immanence states God is *"through all and in all,"* and the definition includes "operating within, indwelling." There is significant similarity between "separate and powerful" and the words associated with transcendence. The same is true for "belonging and relational" to immanence.

With all that in our minds, here is where we are: maybe God displays His image in "male and female" and the broader sense of maleness and femaleness, like "powerful and relational" or "separate and belonging."

God's Attributes and His Image

Finally, consider how God describes Himself. While the following is not a complete list, it represents what the Bible states are the attributes of God. These words describe what it says that He is, His very essence. He is 100% of each of these, always:

Holy, Righteous, Saving, Love, Justice, Judging, Sovereign, Merciful, Gracious, Truth, Wisdom, Self-Existent, Infinite, Eternal, Independent, Compassionate, Relational, Immanent, Immutable, Transcendent, Gentle, Kind, All Powerful (Omnipotent), All Present (Omnipresent), All Knowing (Omniscient)

Keeping it simple, place the above list of attributes into the two categories of maleness and femaleness or "Separate or Powerful" and "Belonging or Relational." Here is how I arranged the words into the categories.

Separate/Powerful (Maleness)	Belonging/Relational (Femaleness)
Holy	Compassionate
Righteous	Saving
Justice – Judging	Merciful
All Powerful (Omnipotent)	All Present (Omnipresent)
All Knowing (Omniscient)	Love
Sovereign	Kind
Truth	Gentle
Wisdom	Gracious
Self-existent	Relational
Infinite / Eternal	
Independent	
Immutable	

The only word that does not easily fit into the categories is "love," primarily because of God's view of love. Love has a powerful as well as a relational component, but I put it on the relational side since it is a critical relational element and more often viewed that way.

Tentative Conclusion: The Image of God

This is certainly not in-depth research, but the idea that the image of God can be described by using the terms of maleness and femaleness is extremely reasonable, especially when you utilize the words that He is separate and powerful, and He is belonging and relational.

There are some wonderful implications if this theory holds true. Most importantly, it provides greater clarity to the roles of men and women and the divine picture of marriage: men and women united in marriage would represent the most complete picture of the image of God, especially if each is doing the roles that God ordained for them.

Before we go any further, I want to be clear about something. When I say His image is reflected in maleness and femaleness, I am not speaking of the physical, but the basic nature. Men primarily reflect God's Separate and Powerful attributes, while women primarily reflect God's Belonging and Relational attributes.

The Image of God in Scripture

The following is not a scholarly treatise on the image of God because that does not align with my desire, credentials, or strengths. On the other hand, if the image of God is best described through maleness and femaleness, Separate and Belonging, or Powerful and Relational, it should not be that difficult to find in God's Word.

Consider the following examples to see if they represent the image of God as proposed. Some examples provide both elements, and others just one.

Micah 6:8

He has shown you, O man, what is good; And
what does the Lord require of you But to do justly,
To love mercy,
And to walk humbly with your God?

Micah 6:8, NKJV

This is one of my favorite verses in the Bible, because of its simple, basic insight into what makes life good. The verse tells you to be separate (do justly) and belonging (love mercy and walk humbly) are what is *good*. A reasonable speculation is that it is good because it reflects God. So, God asks you to be Separate/Powerful (just) and Belonging/Relational (merciful).

Isaiah 57:15

For thus says the High and Lofty One
Who inhabits eternity, whose name is Holy:
"I dwell in the high and holy place,
With him who has a contrite and humble spirit,
To revive the spirit of the humble,
And to revive the heart of the contrite ones."

Isaiah 57:15, NKJV

This verse is spectacular in the way it presents both elements. Even better, this verse is in the context of God telling the nation of Israel that He is willing to forgive and restore them.

Look at the first three lines. Each one is about the power of God or how He is different (separate) from us. He is High and Lofty, inhibiting eternity, Holy, and dwelling in a high and holy place. If you understand some of the reality of that portion of the verse, it initiates a worshipful and humble spirit, because this represents His majesty!

Look at the third line. God first states that He "*dwells in a high and holy place*," then continues to state He dwells with people also. He could have just continued to state how powerful He is and how angry He is with sin (which He has done prior to this verse), but here He wants you to know He is willing to forgive sin.

Equally important is the fact that God states that He dwells in more than one place. He inhabits eternity, dwelling in the high and holy place, but He also dwells with people who have a contrite and humble spirit willing to see their sin and repent of it: Separate/ Powerful, yet Belonging/Relational.

Ephesians 4:15

> But, speaking the truth in love, [we] may grow
> up in all things into Him
> who is the head—Christ—

Ephesians 4:15, NKJV

This verse is foundational to how relationships work best. When you do not seek and share the truth, your relationships suffer. If though, you only seek and share truth, the emphasis would be placed on being Separate/Powerful, because truth is always powerful. That is not what the verse states. You speak "the truth in love," which combines power with what is best for them. So, powerful truth is spoken with the thought of what is best for them: Separate/Powerful yet Belonging/Relational.

2 Timothy 1:7

For God has not given us a spirit of fear, but of power and of love and of a sound mind.

2 Timothy 1:7, NKJV

In Isaiah 57:15 God stated how He is Powerful and Relational. Here Paul tells you that God has given you a combination of power, love, and a sound mind (self-control).

What a wonderful thought for every believer: that God is dedicated to you representing His image properly, so He gives you His Spirit to blossom the fruit of the Spirit in your life. God wants you to display His image in the form of power, love, and self-control instead of fear, so, again: Separate/Powerful, yet Belonging/Relational.

Genesis 1:28

> *Then God blessed them, and God said to them,*
> *"Be fruitful and multiply; fill the earth and*
> *subdue it; have dominion over the fish of the sea,*
> *over the birds of the air, and over every living*
> *thing that moves on the earth."*

Genesis 1:28, NKJV

After God tells you about creating you in His image, He tells you what your purpose is. That purpose has both relational and powerful elements in it. Consider "Be fruitful and multiply". That is obviously a relational element referring to the most intimate options for a man and woman's relationship. And God uses "subdue" and "have dominion" which are power words: Separate/Powerful yet Belonging/Relational.

Genesis 2:16-17 and Genesis 3:8-9

This combination of verses provides an excellent picture of God's image. These two elements are not used in isolation from each, but in combination or proportion as evidenced in Ephesians 4:15. While God related to Adam and Eve, He also provided one clear and powerful boundary for them.

And the Lord God commanded the man, saying,
"Of every tree of the garden you may freely eat;
but of the tree of the knowledge of good and evil
you shall not eat, for in the day that you eat of it
you shall surely die."

Genesis 2:16-17, NKJV

This *powerful* statement was a boundary, and if crossed, it would hurt the relationship. What a good way for you to see how the two interact and support each other. Just like Ephesians 4:15, the power of truth supports the relationship and vice-versa.

But Genesis 3:1-6 tells you Eve was deceived, and Adam ignored the command (it was given to Adam before Eve was created) and they sinned or crossed the boundary. Notice what God did shortly after they sinned:

And they heard the sound of the Lord God
walking in the garden in the cool of the day,
and Adam and his wife hid themselves from the
presence of the Lord God among the trees of the
garden. Then the Lord God called to Adam and
said to him, "Where are you?"

Genesis 3:8-9, NKJV

God did not bring His power or separateness first. He related: "Where are you?" He was asking them not about their location, but if they knew where their hearts or relationship with Him was now. Shortly after this in verses 15-19, God demonstrates His power by judging the serpent, Eve, and Adam. Once again: Separate/ Powerful yet Belonging/Relational.

John 1:1-2, 14

> *In the beginning was the Word, and the Word*
> *was with God, and the Word was God. He was*
> *in the beginning with God . . .*
> *And the Word became flesh and dwelt among us,*
> *and we beheld His glory, the glory as of the only*
> *begotten of the Father, full of grace and truth.*

John 1:1-2, 14, NKJV

Here God refers to the Word (Christ) in two quite different ways. First, "*the Word was with God, and the Word was God.*" Second, "*the Word became flesh and dwelt among us…*"

God provides you a clear picture of His image in the way that He provided a solution to your sin. Christ's death, burial, and resurrection saves you and restores you to the place of ruling that God stated was your purpose back in Genesis 1:28. Christ, the second person of the Trinity, is spoken of as Separate/Powerful, yet Belonging/Relational.

John 3:16-17, 36

> *For God so loved the world that He gave His only begotten Son, that whoever believes in Him should not perish but have everlasting life. For God did not send His Son into the world to condemn the world, but that the world through Him might be saved.*

John 3:16-17, NKJV

These two verses (3:16-17) speak of love, life, and salvation, all very relational items. But now consider the very last verse in the same chapter.

> *He who believes in the Son has everlasting life; and he who does not believe the Son shall not see life, but the wrath of God abides on him.*

John 3:36, NKJV

There are relational items, but some powerful elements are also added. "*He who believes*" can have an everlasting relationship with the Son who provided the solution to your sin. That is a repeat of earlier statements in the chapter. But notice the power addition, he who does not believe will suffer "*the wrath of God.*" Again, you see Separate/Powerful, yet Belonging/Relational.

God's Image in Your Life

You can see how easy it is to show both the powerful and the relational elements in God's Word. While you may not be totally convinced, hopefully it has generated some interest for you to study the idea further.

Clearly, based on all the scriptural references, the image of God has impact on our lives as believers. As we become more intimate in a relationship with Him, we are transformed, and we go from glory to glory over time. The more we focus on Him, the more like Him we become.

We see that Adam was a natural prototype for man, but Jesus is the spiritual prototype through the Resurrection. God loved us so much that in spite of Adam and Eve's actions, which led to the Fall of all mankind, He gave us a second chance to be redeemed through Christ's righteousness, suffering, and sacrifice.

How amazing is it that God describes Himself in ways that reflect our nature as men and women? And yet, He does not say that He is only powerful or only relational. This is a dichotomy that as human beings we may find difficult to comprehend.

Think of people you know. Do you expect them to act powerfully or relationally, but not both? The fact is, you are made in God's image, that means that however He describes himself relates to you.

This is not to dismiss His design for men to Provide, Protect, and Preserve, or for women to Help,

Nurture, and Support. It is only to say that God describes Himself with attributes from both roles. He has not reserved His image for only men or women. All of us reflect His image when we focus on Him and become more intimate in our relationship with Him.

REFLECTIVE QUESTIONS

- Review the words that God uses to describe Himself that are powerful. Describe how you personally think of God in those ways. For example: Holy, He is magnificent, perfect, Moses could not look at Him directly because of His holiness.

  _____

  _____

  _____

  _____

- Review the words that God uses to describe Himself as relational. Describe how you personally think of God in those ways. For example: compassionate; when Jesus saw people who needed to be healed and delivered, He had compassion on them.

  _____

  _____

  _____

  _____

  _____

• Meditate on 1 Corinthians 15:49. What does this reveal to you about God's image naturally and spiritually?

_____

_____

_____

_____

• Based on 2 Corinthians 3:18, think of your life. How are you being transformed from glory to glory?

_____

_____

_____

_____

• Study and meditate on the beauty and reality of Genesis, in the first 12 chapters. Record your revelation of wisdom in those chapters. What truths can you apply to your life?

_____

_____

_____

_____

_____

GOD'S IMAGE IN MEN AND WOMEN

Since God had a specific purpose for mankind on the earth, it makes sense that God would design man and woman to fulfill that purpose. In Genesis chapter two, God provides insight into the design of men and women. Earlier you saw some of the design of man and woman, but here is more detail. Starting with man, look at the following verses and see the specific reasons God created him.

> No shrub or plant of the field was yet in the earth, and no herb of the field had yet sprouted, for the LORD God had not caused it to rain on the earth, and there was no man to cultivate the ground, but a mist (fog, dew, vapor) used to rise from the land and water the entire surface of the ground— then the LORD God formed [that is, created the body of] man from the dust of the ground, and breathed into his nostrils the breath of life; and the man became a living being [an individual complete in body and spirit]. So

the Lord God took the man [He had made] and
settled him in the Garden of Eden to cultivate
and keep it.

Genesis 2:5-7, 15, AMP

Creation of Man

When you look at Genesis 2:5 and 15 from other translations, it's clear that man's design was to till the ground.

Genesis 2:5

". . . there was no man to till the ground..."
(NKJV)
". . . there was no man to work the ground..."
(NIV)

Genesis 2:15

God put the man in the garden to
". . . tend and keep it." (NKJV)
". . . work it and take care of it." (NIV)
". . . dress it and to keep it." (KJV)
". . . cultivate it and keep it." (NASB)

These verses are not difficult to understand. Man was created and designed *to till the ground* . . . and . . . *tend and keep* . . . the Garden. Of course, every man is not literally working in a garden or farming, so there is a broader implication. The first word of verse 15 is translated as tend, work, dress, or cultivate. The Hebrew definition is: labor, work, serve, till, and sometimes implies enslavement.

Webster's Dictionary definitions are:
- Tend: to be in charge of, manage, operate, to take care of
- Work: physical or mental effort directed toward doing or making something
- Dress: to till and cultivate land, apply fertilizer, prune, and trim
- Cultivate: till, prepare land for growth; plant, tend, harvest, or improve (plants) by labor and skill

The broader implication is that all the words are primarily about work or labor. Now look at the second word in verse 15 is translated "keep" or "take care of".

The Hebrew definition is: have charge of, protect, preserve, watch, guard, or restrain

Webster's Dictionary definitions are:
- Keep – to protect, guard, or defend; to have, take charge or care of, to look after, maintain for use

- Take care – careful or serious attention, protective or supervisory control, to provide physical needs, help, or comfort

When guarding and protecting that obviously requires labor, effort, or work, but they also have a relational element to them.

Obviously, in this day and age, not all men are in their backyard or on their land tilling the ground to support their families. Here is the broader implication: the first word of verse 15 is translated as tend, work, dress or cultivate. The Hebrew definition is labor, work, serve, till and sometimes implies enslavement. The second word is translated, *keep* or *take care of.* In Hebrew the definition is *have charge of, guard* or *restrain.* These definitions indicate that labor, effort and work is required, but they also have a relationship element. Let's look at that relational element for a moment.

> *And the Lord God said, "It is not good that man should be alone; I will make him a helper comparable to him." Out of the ground the Lord God formed every beast of the field and every bird of the air, and brought them to Adam to see what he would call them. And whatever Adam called each living creature, that was its name. So Adam gave names to all cattle, to the birds of the*

air, and to every beast of the field. But for Adam
there was not found a helper comparable to him
. . .

Genesis 2:18-20, NKJV

God stated that man's *aloneness* was not good.
God did not speak for Adam and say, "He was lonely,"
although some preachers may indicate that. *The point is*
God saw Adam's need and met that need. This is significant
because many men are blissfully ignorant of their need
for a helper. By God's mercy a man wakes up and sees
the benefit that God provides him through his wife.

Finally, God's design of man included oneness
with woman.

Therefore a man shall leave his father and mother
and be joined to his wife, and they shall become
one flesh.

Genesis 2:24, NKJV

Man's need for suitable companionship clearly
shows that God sees the combination of man and woman's
design as good. You will see why that combination is
so important when you learn about the foundation of
man and woman's design. The implication is man and
woman's designs complement each other.

Consider a farming metaphor, man is designed
to provide, protect, and preserve the seed. He is

designed to work, cultivate, keep, take care of, manage, and develop what is planted. And all this done best in companionship with woman, because his design needs compatible help, suitable companionship in the process. That companionship element with woman is encouraged when God states that he is to separate from mother and father and be joined as one with a woman.

Why is the design of man so important to know? Because not knowing or paying attention to the design of something increases the probability of misuse. Consider a time you decided to use a butter knife as a screwdriver. You can make it work, but that is not what it was designed to do. Knowing your design is critical. Otherwise you do not know if you are using it properly.

Men, you are designed for *work and activity*. Three words that adequately describe a man's design include *Provide, Protect and Preserve*. The design of man works best when a woman is included, and vice-versa. Let's explore the creation of woman.

Creation of Woman

> *And the Lord God said, "It is not good that man should be alone; I will make him a helper comparable to him."*

Genesis 2:18, NKJV

God said it was "Not good that man should be alone."

God wanted a "A helper comparable to him."
So, God made exactly what man needed: Woman.

And the Lord God caused a deep sleep to fall on Adam, and he slept; and He took one of his ribs, and closed up the flesh in its place. Then the rib which the Lord God had taken from man He made into a woman, and He brought her to the man. And Adam said: "This is now bone of my bones and flesh of my flesh; she shall be called Woman, because she was taken out of Man."

Genesis 2:21-23, NKJV

God had clear reasoning for creating woman. She is to be a helper to man. Other versions say the helper will be *suitable*, *meet*, or *as his counterpart*. And men, God clearly says you need a helper.

You may have the opinion, as do many, that the role and value of a helper is less than the one who is helped. Satan wants you to think that! His lie is that if women do not have the same role as men, they must not have the same value. It is the same lie he tells people everywhere: if you do not have a large or prestigious role, it means you are less of a person or less valuable.

To enlighten your perspective, let's think about how God uses the word *helper*. The Hebrew word for helper is *ezer*. In the Bible the word is translated as *help* nineteen times and *helpmeet* two times. *Ezer* means help, support, aid and it often designates assistance like we see in Genesis 2:18. Helper is generally used to refer to God as we see in the Psalms.

> *I will lift up my eyes to the hills—From whence comes my help? My help comes from the LORD, Who made heaven and earth.*

Psalm 121:1-2, NKJV

Since God describes Himself as a helper, this could not be a demeaning term.

Women, being a helper is a high calling and exactly how God designed you. Essentially, as a helper, you look at life through God's eyes and act like Him because it elevates your thinking beyond yourself. Not only that, God designed you as a helper who is *comparable* or *suitable*. In the English suitable means, *appropriate, a fit, adapted to a use or purpose, satisfying propriety, able, qualified.*

What great words to put on your personal resume! You are described the same way God describes Himself. Where men are designed to Provide, Protect and Preserve, women are designed with an emphasis and strength to relate, including all the facets that requires. God uniquely created women to Help, Nurture, and Support.

Going back to the farming metaphor, women are designed to help, nurture, and support the seed.

A woman bears, births, assists, aids, and gives relief to what was planted. Like man, a woman does not do this alone, because she is the complementary companion to help man and his aloneness, which is often unrecognized by man. Finally, a woman's design is best utilized in combination with man's design, joining in complementary oneness.

Women, you are designed with an emphasis and strength to *relate* and all the many facets that requires. Whatever you endeavor, whether leading or following, when you use your innate ability to relate, you focus on your strength. I ask every woman leader who I coach, to consider leading with their relational design instead of trying to be powerful.

Overall, the words *Help, Nurture and Support* reasonably describe a woman's design.

These two designs fit together to represent God in the Earth. What a privilege to be designed in His image with specific roles to fulfill.

Balance and Proportion

While God has created this perfect design in terms of roles and the interaction of men and women, God's image and purpose for men and women has been distorted in our dying world. You see this everywhere, including relationships, business, and even church.

Men are viewed as powerful, and women relational, as though women are less valuable. Nothing is further from the truth as we see it in God's Word. In scripture God reveals Himself as both powerful and relational. These two elements are not used in isolation from each other, but properly proportioned as we see in various scriptures.

Ephesians speaks of Christ as the head of the church, indicating power, yet He speaks the truth in love, which is relational.

> *but, speaking the truth in love, may grow up in all things into Him who is the head—Christ.*

Ephesians 4:15, NKJV

John indicates that the Word is God and yet the Word became flesh and dwelt among us. Almighty God, full of glory and truth came to dwell among us and have a relationship with us.

> *In the beginning was the Word, and the Word was with God, and the Word was God. He was in the beginning with God . . .*
> *And the Word became flesh and dwelt among us, and we beheld His glory, the glory as of the only begotten of the Father, full of grace and truth.*

John 1:1-2, 14

Again, here is what the prophet Isaiah says of God. God is the high and lofty one, He inhabits eternity, and

His name is Holy. And yet in the latter part of the verse, He dwells with people to revive the spirit of the humble and contrite ones.

> *For thus says the High and Lofty One*
> *Who inhabits eternity, whose name is Holy:*
> *"I dwell in the high and holy place,*
> *With him who has a contrite and humble spirit,*
> *To revive the spirit of the humble,*
> *And to revive the heart of the contrite ones."*

Isaiah 57:15, NKJV

God is both powerful and relational. Neither attribute is less important than the other.

God's Image in the Workplace

The thought of God's image appearing in the workplace may seem unusual to you based on your experience, but thinking about the design and function of men and women does apply to work situations. Especially when you look at integration of design of men and women and their roles in the workplace. Am I saying that only men can run corporations and women must be administrative assistants? Not at all.

In the scenario below, examine the relationships described to look for indicators of God's design and His image, then answer the questions at the end.

Scenario

Jones Marketing Group started out as a local family-owned business in St. Louis, Missouri. Edwin Jones founded the business at the young age of 25, after working for a large marketing firm right out of college. He was a visionary for what the business could become, yet a micro-manager in some ways. Most of the time that he ran the company he was looking over the shoulder of people who were charged with managing Finance, Marketing, Operations, and Public Relations.

Here's a timeline of events that occurred during the building of the business, and the personalities involved.

Year One: Edwin Jones leaves his high-paying position in a large marketing firm located in New York City, and moves home to St. Louis to found Jones Marketing Group. His wife, Margaret supports him in the firm, serving in multiple functions.

Year Three: Margaret retires when their twins are born, and Edwin hires a distant cousin, Amos Roundtree to take over Margaret's duties. By this time the firm has grown quite a bit, so they are looking to add others to the executive suite.

Year Five: Amos has taken over as Director of Operations, Mark Adams, Edwin's brother-in-law has filled the spot of Director of Public Relations, John Jones, Edwin's brother heads up Marketing and Ed Whitley is the Director of Finance.

Year Twenty: Ed Whitley leaves as Director of Finance because he wants a job with more autonomy and responsibility. Miriam Bozley, Edwin's sister leaves her career as a CPA for a large accounting firm to take over as Director of Finance.

*****

When Miriam joins the firm, she notices that the Marketing and Operations Directors were at odds with each other about 80 percent of the time, which is hurting the company's financial performance. John Jones, Marketing Director and a high-drive, focused individual is always pushing for new programs and more employees. He is not detail-oriented and gets a lot of push-back from Amos, the Operations Director. Since John is Edwin's older brother, Edwin usually sides with him in disagreements between John and Amos.

Amos is meticulous and soft-spoken, but an astute businessman, whose attention to detail has served the firm well. The Human Resources function is under his management, so whenever he has to intervene in disputes, he is keen on listening with an open mind and not jumping to conclusions. Because of this he has created a great amount of trust and respect within the organization. He is viewed as someone whose goal is to serve the needs of the company and do what is best for long-term operations.

Since Miriam is new to the firm, she doesn't say anything right away. She is ultimately responsible for identifying issues in the firm that are impacting financial performance. So, she decides to focus her attention on documenting what she observes before bringing up issues to Amos or John.

Three months later, Miriam feels she has enough evidence to show how the conflict between John and Amos is hurting the company. She wants to handle this situation delicately, so she sets up individual meetings with all of the Directors in the company to review improvements that could be made. She explains to Edwin that she wants to meet with all of them first, before meeting with him, because she thinks the Directors might each have valuable input for making the firm better. Edwin reluctantly agrees because on some level he knows he has a tendency to try to control everything and he needs to let people do their jobs.

The meeting with Mark Adams, Director of Public Relations is uneventful. Mark's job is more externally focused, and he works well with Amos, always collaborating with him about his vision for PR and employee resources required. They meet once a month.

Amos made sure he had all the documentation that Miriam asked for prior to the meeting. The conversation went like this.

"Miriam, it's great to have you on board. I'm glad you are meeting with each of us so we can support you with any information or documentation you need."

"Thanks Amos, I appreciate you saying that. I want to have a good working relationship will all our leaders so I can help direct us to financial success," Miriam said with a smile. "I wanted to discuss some of the Marketing initiatives that you asked John to delay. Can you explain your reasoning?"

"Sure. The first one was a Golf Tournament that John wanted to sponsor. Looking at who would be attending, we wouldn't be attracting any new clients, and the ones that he wanted to invite, have not really done that much work with us. Also, he didn't indicate that we would be able to get any leverage from the attendees' contacts. When he showed me how much it would cost, and the amount of labor on our part. It did not make sense to me."

Miriam nodded her head in agreement and said, "That makes sense."

They talked over one other project, then ended the meeting.

Miriam walked to John's office and tapped on the door frame. "You ready to meet?" she asked.

"Sure!" he said as he stood up and extended his hand to shake hers.

"Thanks for meeting with me today. I look forward to working with you to build and sustain this company," she said.

"Of course!" John exclaimed. "Have a seat."

Knowing John to be a strong and opinionated personality she started by letting him expound on his marketing plans. Several times he mentioned that Amos was holding them back because of his fear of failure. Miriam did not react but made a note of the comments.

Toward the end of the meeting John said, "You know at the end of the day, we are all here to grow the company and create a powerhouse that dominates our industry. The fact is, it takes money and human resources to do that. All I'm trying to do build this business as fast as I can."

Miriam nodded and said, "I appreciate your candor and drive to grow the company."

Miriam left his office and went back to hers. Lots of ideas were swirling in her head, so she closed the door to process all that she had heard from the key players. It wasn't really her responsibility to help John and Amos see eye-to-eye, but she knew she needed to manage that to move the company in a new and more profitable direction.

The next day Miriam had a meeting with Edwin.

Edwin started the conversation by saying, "Tell me the results of your meetings."

Miriam explained, "As I suspected there is a chasm in philosophy between Amos and John."

"Oh, I know," Edwin replied. "I need to get Amos to take some more risks."

Miriam asked, "What do you mean exactly?"

"You can't make more money and expand unless you are willing to spend it."

Miriam said, "That's true to an extent, but we need to take calculated risks at this point in the growth of the firm."

"Yes, yes," he said impatiently. "Let's stay in touch regarding the financials and how John plans to build the firm."

Miriam realized he had pretty much dismissed her from the discussion. Feeling no resolution from this meeting, she decided it was best to continue the discussion later.

Scenario Questions

1. In the scenario, look at power versus relational. Where do you see the attitude of power displayed? Where do you see relational attributes displayed?

_____

_____

_____

2. Who in the scenario shows support of others? What did they do to indicate that?

_____

_____

_____

_____

3. How could those who display that attitude of power become more effective if they were more relational? What would you suggest they do to change?

_____

_____

_____

4. How would the changes noted in question 3 improve the company overall?

_____

_____

_____

Summary

When you look closely at God's image and how it relates to the design for men and women and the balance and proportion of His image in His Word, you can begin to see it displayed in the Earth in various scenarios. God's image is implanted in our lives if only we stop and observe and acknowledge it. He is powerful yet relational, which we don't always find in people. As you journey through life, observe how you demonstrate a representation of His power and His incredibly loving relationship with us.

REFLECTIVE QUESTIONS

- God saw Adam's need to not be alone. How does women's creation and design fulfill that need?

  _____

  _____

  _____

  _____

- How does the notion of God referring to Himself as a *helper* impact your thinking about His design for women?

  _____

  _____

  _____

  _____

- What strengths do you see in the way that God designed women?

  _____

  _____

  _____

  _____

- Regarding the topic of Balance and Control, what new thinking did that create for you regarding Who God is?

_____

_____

_____

_____

REFLECTING OR DISTORTING GOD'S IMAGE

Though we were planned and made in God's image and relationships between men and women were intended to follow in His divine design, we don't always represent Him as well as we could. Let's explore how we can reflect His image and what we do to distort His image. By reflecting His image we actually serve as a better witness for Him in our daily lives.

Reflecting His Image

Satan is the author of confusion, right? So, what would he want you to be most confused about? My speculation is that he does not want you to be clear about who God is. Satan wants your thinking to be fuzzy and distorted about how God thinks, feels, and acts. That includes a lack of clarity about His image. If he can create doubt in your mind about the true nature of God, then you are much more vulnerable to temptation.

The evidence of that statement is in Genesis 3 with Satan's response to Eve saying she could not eat of the Tree of Life due to God's command to Adam and her.

> *Then the serpent said to the woman, "You will not surely die. For God knows that in the day you eat of it your eyes will be opened, and you will be like God, knowing good and evil."*

Genesis 3:4-5, NKJV

Satan, as he always does, tries to convince us that God does not have our best at heart, that He is not who He says He is. Satan tries to put doubt in our hearts and distort our thinking about God's true image.

Living as God desires means that you are reflecting, however minutely, the image of God.

God's image is ingrained in you and every man and woman and cannot be hidden.

Sometimes you reflect it in ways that are surprisingly true. Other times, you distort it badly, causing more harm than you know.

The image of God has much broader application and implications than you might think. It is an integral part of everyday life. Any relationship, be it business or personal, formal or informal, long-term or short-term, will have a power element and a relational element involved. In fact, God's image is seen everywhere, so long as you look for it.

God's Image in Song

Below I have listed an example of God's image being described in an old hymn, *Great is Thy Faithfulness*.

> *Great is Thy faithfulness Oh God my Father*
> *There is no shadow of turning with Thee*
> *Thou changest not, Thy compassion they fail not*
> *As Thou has been Thou forever will be.*
>
> *Great is Thy faithfulness, great is Thy faithfulness,*
> *Morning by morning new mercies I see.*
> *All I have needed Thy hand hath provided.*
> *Great is Thy faithfulness, Lord, unto me.*
>
> *Summer and winter springtime and harvest,*
> *Sun moon and stars in their courses above,*
> *Join with all nature in manifold witness,*
> *To Thy great faithfulness mercy and love.*
>
> *Pardon for sin and a peace that endureth,*
> *Thine own dear presence to cheer and to guide.*
> *Strength for today and bright hope for tomorrow,*
> *Blessings all mine with ten thousand beside.*

Looking at these lyrics, one powerful element that stands out is *All I have needed thy hand hath provided*. God can and will provide for any need you have. His power is sufficient, and He uses that power because He is relating to you, His child.

> *Consider the ravens, for they neither sow nor*
> *reap, which have neither storehouse nor barn;*
> *and God feeds them. Of how much more value*
> *are you than the birds?*

Luke 12:24, NKJV

Think of *pardon for sin and peace that endureth.* That represents God's power by pardoning sin and providing enduring peace. Isaiah speaks about pardon.

> *Let the wicked forsake his way,And the*
> *unrighteous man his thoughts;*
> *Let him return to the* LORD,
> *And He will have mercy on him;*
> *And to our God,*
> *For He will abundantly pardon.*

Isaiah 55:7, NKJV

Here is a scripture about the peace that only God can give:

> *and the peace of God, which surpasses*
> *all understanding, will guard your hearts and*
> *minds through Christ Jesus.*

Philippians 4:7, NKJV

Let's see what the Bible says about, *Strength for today and bright hope for tomorrow.*

*But those who wait on the Lord Shall renew their strength; They shall mount up with **wings** like **eagles**, They shall run and not be weary, They shall walk and not faint.*

Isaiah 40:31, NKJV

Here is what God promised to the Israelites who were in captivity in Babylon.

For I know the thoughts that I think toward you, says the Lord, thoughts of peace and not of evil, to give you a future and a hope.

Jeremiah 29:11, NKJV

In *Great is Thy Faithfulness* you can see both God's steadfast and unchanging power and His tender mercy as He walks in close fellowship with His children. In other Christian songs, you see just one element. Be careful to remember that both elements represent who God is. For example, it might be easier for you to sing about God's love for you than about His power and majesty. When you only sing about one element and not the other, you may be allowing a distortion of God's image in your mind.

Another place that both elements are shown is in the unwelcome complaints and grumbling that worship/music leaders endure in some measure. "You need more old hymns about fearing God (Power). Those songs we are singing are too personal and disrespectful, as though Jesus was our boyfriend (Relational)."

Or conversely, "Those hymns are so dry and distant (Separate). I wish we would sing something about God being with me in my own personal trials (Belonging)."

When you have access to a hymnal, or listen to Christian music, or sing in church, see if you can identify if one or both elements are in a song.

God's Image in Movies

Most science fiction, westerns, war films, or action/adventure movies will be more Separate or Powerful. They appeal to power instincts because they are full of action, missions, and quest. People or characters in the movie must be saved and protected. The theme presents a constant battle between good and evil.

The Relational or Belonging movies include categories like comedies, romantic comedies, love stories, dramas, and musicals. The themes or plots revolve around relationships between people, which are more driven by dialogue and personal interactions between and among people. Obviously, the relational element is primary, but note that power is often introduced to create a setback in the relationship.

But both Power and Belonging will be evident in every movie, and the best films emphasizing them at the best time. Consider the classic *Star Wars* films. At first glance, they seem to only be Sci-fi action films, full of flashy lightsabers and blaster battles between good and evil.

But they also have the element of relationships to allow the viewer to become part of the movie. The dialogue, timeless romance, and intensely emotional family conflict make the movie real, because the viewer needs to relate to the characters.

Darth Vader, the dark villain, turns out to be the "dark father" of Luke Skywalker, the young hero for the *good* side. A love-hate relationship between Han Solo, the independent and rogue pilot, and Princess Leia, the feisty warrior princess for good, emerges. On top of that, Luke Skywalker and Princess Leia turn out to be brother and sister, a fact the producers of the famous initial trilogy cleverly left until one of the later movies.

These movies contain battles between good and evil, and exhilarating scenes where each side wields their *power*. Some of the characters are *separated* from others, because of their arrogant and rogue nature. The *Star Wars* movies provide plenty examples of God's image from both sides of the equation without expressly saying it.

God's Image in Religions

Religions often distort God's image by focusing too much (or even exclusively) on one element. Separate or Powerful examples are Islam, Deism, Agnosticism, Animism and African Tribal religions. Any religion that focuses on fear of God (this is different than the fear of the Lord, found in the Bible in Psalm 111:10) or see Him as some distant force has missed who God says He is. Belonging or Relational examples would be Mormonism (relationship/family-centered), Human Potential Movement, New Age Movement, and forms of Hinduism and Buddhism.

Sadly, even Christianity is skewed when denominations emphasize one element to the exclusion of the other. When the emphasis is on the rules, knowledge, and traditions, it tends to be more Separate or Powerful. But there is also the other side that emphasizes a concept of love without teaching the consequences of sin and the fear of God.

Due to our sin nature and the influence of Satan we can easily distort the image of God, causing us to worship what is not God, which pleases Satan because we don't see God for who He really is.

Image of God in Personality Tests

You can even see God's image in personality traits. The words in the following table are part of several different personality tests. When you consider the definition of each word it is rather easy to put them into Separate or Belonging categories. Some of the words have elements of both, but the way they are arranged in the chart is the primary use of the word.

This list is not based on intense research, only an example that you can find the image of God even in personality tests. Instead of just putting the words into two categories, you can use these lists to estimate which of the two elements you think best describes your personality. If you want to do that, just go down each column and pick the words that you believe fit you the best.

Separate/Powerful	Belonging/Relational
Productive	Distracter
Conspirator	Peacemaker
Blamer	Placater
Confrontational	Perceiver
Thinker	Feeler
Intuitive	Senser
Lion	Golden Retriever
Intimidating	Relational
Domineering	Compliant
Introvert	Extrovert
Beaver	Otter
Independent	Dependent
Judger	Encourager
Total:	**Total:**

Almost every word in the Separate and Powerful best describes me. My wife, Louie, and my friends would agree. Having a preference or leaning toward one column is not only natural, it is most likely, because we are not perfect like God. It's also part of both our design and development.

Just like movies and religions, your personality will tend to be represented by one column more than the other. But that does not mean you will always act or be exclusively that way. Personality tests most often measure preferences more than the way you are designed. That means your preferences may or may not align with your design. For example, some men may pick more of the Belonging or Relational words and some women may pick more Separate or Powerful words. Why is that? Because we can develop tendencies and preferences that may accentuate or be different from our design.

Personalities in Relationships

Joan and Richard have been married for five years. They have a four-year-old daughter, Ashley. Joan is an attorney for a large local law firm, who works from her law firm's office fifty percent of the time and works from home the rest of the time. Sometimes she has to work at night and long hours, depending on her workload. Richard is a Chiropractor who works part-time. He studied to be a chef at one time, so he does most of the cooking for the family. They have planned their working situation so that they do not have to send their daughter to daycare. As you read the scenario, make a note of the personality characteristics in the chart below that you see in Joan and Richard individually.

Separate/Powerful	Belonging/Relational
Productive	Distracter
Conspirator	Peacemaker
Blamer	Placater
Confrontational	Perceiver
Thinker	Feeler
Intuitive	Senser
Lion	Golden Retriever
Intimidating	Relational
Domineering	Compliant
Introvert	Extrovert
Beaver	Otter
Independent	Dependent
Judger	Encourager

Scenario

It's a rainy Monday. Joan is not looking forward to braving the flooded streets in their town, but duty calls. The senior partner in her firm has called an important meeting for all the attorneys who work there. The firm has landed a huge case and they need everyone to work on it.

Richard sees the distress on her face as she prepares to face the weather conditions and a likely stressful meeting.

"You worried about the streets, Hun?"

"Of course!" she says. "Wouldn't you be?"

"You just looked stressed out," he says in a kind tone of voice.

"Yeah, I am. I'm going to drive across town, avoiding a lot of people who don't think straight when they are driving in the rain, only to attend a meeting, where everyone will be vying for top position on this case."

"Well, maybe you won't have to fight to be chosen. You've definitely proven yourself there," Richard tried to encourage her.

"Thanks, Rich," she said with a smile.

Just then, Ashley walked in the room with her favorite raincoat on. "I'm ready to go to, Daddy!"

Suddenly a broad smile came across Joan's face. She turned all her attention to Ashley, and said, "That is the cutest coat I have ever seen. Do you know why?"

Ashley put her hands in the air as if to say, "I don't know."

"Because *you* are wearing it," Joan said with a laugh as she gave Ashley a big hug.

Richard smiled and said, "Let's go get in the car Ashley, we don't want to be late for school. Tell Mom good-bye."

Richard and Ashely left and Joan spent a few minutes reading and writing in her devotional journal before leaving.

Joan arrived in the office's main conference room and noted who was sitting by whom to determine the "lay of the land" for the meeting. All the senior partners and people vying for partner in the firm were sitting at one end of the huge conference table, with laptops and legal pads at the ready for the meeting.

James, one of the lawyers had been briefed on the case ahead of time and was busy doing last-minute research for the meeting. He did not even look up when Joan arrived.

"Good morning everyone," she said in a cheery voice. "I hope none of you ran into trouble driving through the flood today."

"Not at all," said Elliott the firm's senior partner who had called the meeting.

June, one of the legal assistants said, "I did okay Joan. I just avoided the highway, to avoid the idiots," she said with a laugh.

Joan smiled and said, "There are always plenty of those."

Joan found a seat at the opposite end from the senior partner and quietly unpacked her laptop and notebooks to prepare for the meeting.

Elliott started the meeting in his normal serious tone and explained an overview of the case. With a stern look on his face he looked at everyone at the table as he told them that this case had to take priority over everything. And he reminded them not to whine to him, just figure out how to do what they needed to do to support the firm. He assured everyone that there would be rewards for those who were ready to *play ball.*

The meeting went on for a couple of hours. Joan felt her competitive spirit rise as she noticed the other attorneys in the room trying to show how smart they are. She took a few deep breaths to remain calm, and not give away her desperate need to succeed at the firm. This was not just to satisfy her personal need for achievement, but to provide for Ashley's education. Joan and Richard were determined to be able to send Ashley to private school, so that she could get into a good college. Joan's parents did not save for her college, so she put herself through college and law school. She did not want the same for her daughter.

At the end of the meeting Joan was absolutely exhausted from the long meeting and the internal struggles she was processing during the meeting. She knew it would look best if she stayed at the office the rest of the day. She called Richard and asked if he could be available for Ashley during the afternoon today. He said he would be glad to rearrange some patients to accommodate her need to stay at the office.

Joan arrived home around 6:00 pm, just in time to sit down for dinner. Ashley was in a fussy mood and started whining about having to eat broccoli with her dinner.

Joan wasn't in the mood for whining, and said, "Ashley, you need to eat that, because your dad worked hard to make this meal. Broccoli is good for you. It will make you smarter."

Ashley continued to whine, and Joan said firmly, "That's enough of that, just eat it."

"Okay Mommy," she complied.

Richard looked lovingly at Ashley and said, "Thanks baby."

Ashley looked at him compliantly and nodded her head.

After dinner, Richard hopped up, took up all the dishes and cleaned the kitchen.

Then he herded Ashley to her room to get ready for bed and the bedtime story. Joan came in the room to read her the story. Joan let Ashley choose the book she wanted for them to read.

After the story, Joan tucked Ashley into her bed and said, "Sweet dreams, Miss Ashley."

Ashley laughed and said, "I'm not a Miss Ashley! I'm only four!"

Joan couldn't contain herself and started laughing at her daughter's almost defiant statement. Joan kissed her daughter's forehead and quietly left the room.

When Joan came out of the room, Richard was glued to his laptop. She could tell he was working on the family finances.

She thought to herself, "I am lucky that my husband is dogged about managing our finances. I may bring in more money than him, but that works because I am more driven to make a name for myself, but I'm not into details like that."

Since Richard was so focused on what he was doing she decided not to disturb him. She went into her home office and started a Zoom call with a colleague from work to debrief the meeting they had that morning. They discussed the case and office politics for a couple of hours.

When she emerged, Richard was watching his favorite Sports News program.

"Sorry I stayed in the office so long," she apologized. "I got carried away talking to James, which is a rare opportunity. He has the best read on office politics and always knows more facts and figures about cases than anyone else."

"I get that. I was buried in our finances, anyway, having a good time with my spreadsheet. I'm good on my own," he said with a smile.

"Yes you are," she said.

Scenario Questions

1. In the chart below, for each person listed, indicate a behavior you noticed in the scenario and record it in the middle column. Then on the right indicate whether the behavior is Powerful or Relational.

_____

_____

_____

_____

2. Thinking of the office relationships, how
    is powerful and relational impacting the
    relationships?

_____

_____

_____

_____

3. Look at the items you listed for Joan and
    Richard. How is powerful and relational
    helping and hurting Joan and Richard's
    relationship?

_____

_____

_____

_____

4. Based on what you identified about Joan
    and Richard, what impact will they have on
    Ashley?

_____

_____

_____

_____

_____

_____

5. What can you apply from the scenario to your
    own life, including work, spouse or family
    relationships?

_____

_____

_____

_____

Distorting His Image

Thinking about God's image, a slide switch can help you understand the Separate/Powerful with the Belonging/Relational elements of the image of God. Having the picture of the switch helps you see how easy it is to distort the image of God and His designs for us.

The Relationship Slide Switch

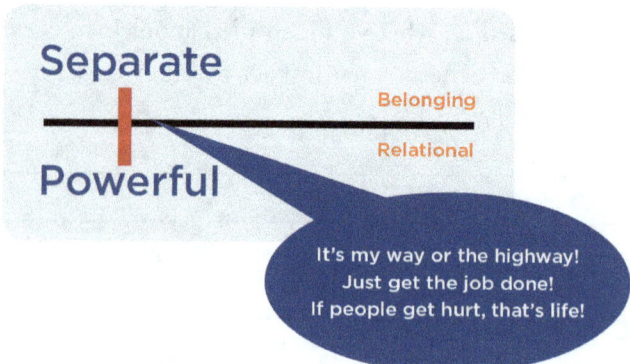

On the graphic, the red bar on the black line can move to the right or left and be anywhere on the line. The red bar is shown on the Separate or Powerful side, so the words are bigger. But the red bar can move to the Relating side also. If it were on the other side, then those words would be bigger. So, your behavior can be anywhere on the horizontal line, even at the extreme left or right.

- If the red bar is more on the left, you display more Separate or Powerful behavior
- If the red bar is more on the right, you display more Belonging or Relational behavior

Your relationships are heavily impacted by Results and Relating. If you overuse either one, you hurt the relationship. God uses the perfect level of Results and Relating as He works with us.

Think about how you tend to act in most situations. Do you focus more energy on being Separate or Powerful?

If you do, statements like, "It's my way or the highway!" "Just get the job done!" or, "If people get hurt, that's life" could be used of that behavior when at the extreme left side.

Your actions would be more dominant, aggressive, vocal, and maybe even angry toward others. You can also be quiet, and still be on the Powerful side. It is not about loud and vocal, it is about focusing on work and activities, but not as much on people. Power or Results are the priority more than relationships. You relate to people, but results are the primary focus; relationships are secondary. The further to the left on the switch, the more focus on power or results and less on *getting along* with people.

Do you focus more energy on Belonging or Relational, the right side?

At the extreme right, it is like saying, "Let's just get along!" "Unity is all we need!" or, "I just want everyone to feel good about each other!"

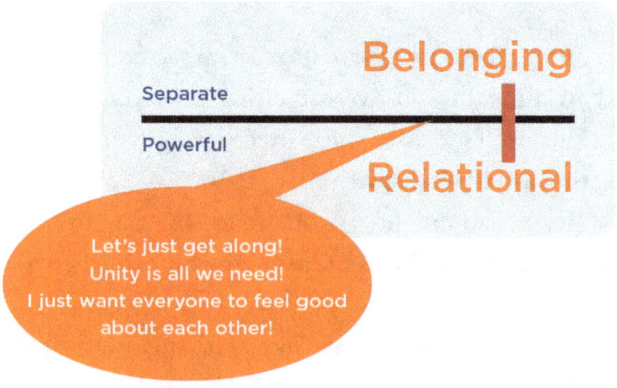

You do not like to make situations or relationships uncomfortable for anyone, and you might even say you agree with someone when you really do not.

Relational energy values people, not to the exclusion of results, but as a priority above results. The further to the right, the less energy for results, and more energy is placed on relating to people. When on the relational side, manipulation is often the way to control people. For example, if you want to persuade someone, you will not try to force your idea on them. You would manipulate, so they do not see that you are attempting to get your way. On the powerful/results side, force and fear are used for control.

Summary

Again, most people fall on one side or the other, focus on results or focus on relating. No matter what your design, God wants you to depend on Him to accurately reflect that design and His image.

> *For God has not given us a spirit of fear, but of power and of love and of a sound mind.*

2 Timothy 1:7, NKJV

Values

Let's look at how our values affect how we respond. If you are more on the Separate or Powerful side, you probably ignore some important people values.

Consider moving the switch more toward Relational by asking yourself questions like those listed below.

1. What principle about belonging and relating to people am I ignoring?
2. Am I caring for and about others?
3. Am I considering the power of gentleness?
4. Am I using the truth with mercy?
5. Am I pursuing their best?

When you are on the Separate side, people are not the focus, results are. But remember: people get results. Results seldom just happen; it takes people to generate the results needed. This means finding better ways to relate to people will help you achieve the desired results.

The Relationship Slide Switch

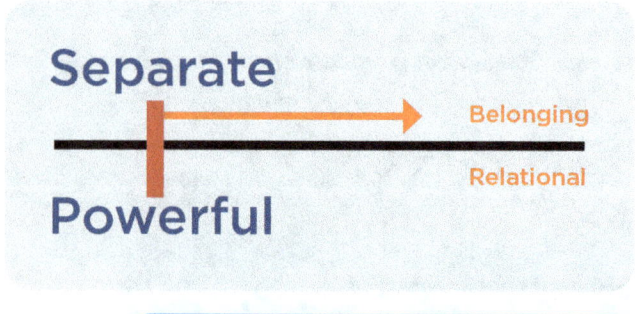

Gentleness reduces barriers, force builds them. Use truth with mercy.

It is not necessarily wrong to push people in order to get results. If done too often, however, rebellion is likely. People comply with force, but only to a point. Compliance is not what you want; you want the complete strengths of the people to show up to help get the desired results. Gentleness, grace, and freedom reduces barriers. Find ways to add a more Belonging or Relational attitudes and actions into your life.

Alternatively, if your tendency is Belonging or Relational you may ignore boundaries or principles about getting results. You may neglect the opportunity to stand up and do what is right even when others are not. That means you need to move the switch toward Separate and Powerful by asking questions like:

The Relationship Slide Switch

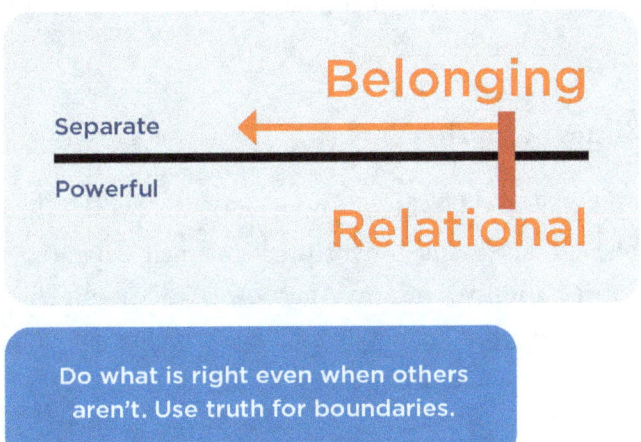

1. What principle about Results or maintaining boundaries am I ignoring?
2. Am I doing what is right, standing on good values?
3. Am I relating without violating my values?
4. Am I using truth for boundaries?
5. Am I pursuing their best?

When on the Belonging or Relational side your focus is on people – you want to get along. Sometimes the other person in the relationship may be on the Power side taking advantage of you. Or they could be on the Belonging side with you, which may mean values, boundaries, or truth are ignored. Neither situation is good for the health of a relationship.

Moving the switch more toward Separate or Powerful takes strength and courage, which is available in abundance from the Holy Spirit.

Values Scenario

Mary and David have been married 32 years. Their son is disabled and lives with them, their daughter is married and lives nearby. Mary owns a local gift shop and David has retired from his corporate job as a manager at a manufacturing firm.

Read the scenario below, then answer the questions.

It's Monday morning, Mary is running late to open the shop and calls her husband, who is at a Rotary Club meeting with their son.

"David, can you go to the store to open. I got a late start, and the dogs are a mess. MaryAnne doesn't have a key, so I don't want her waiting outside to open. I still have to stop by the hardware store to get the fixtures for the contractor to hang the new shelves."

"James and I will head over there now."

"I'm sorry, I hate to interrupt your day. I hope you are not mad at me," Mary replies.

"Not at all, we will go and handle it for you."

"Thank you so much, you guys are the best," Mary gushed.

"Okay. We are on our way over."

"Thank you so much, I love you guys!"

Mary hangs up the phone wondering how David really feels. He never shows emotion. David thinks nothing of the conversation, only thinking of his task to open the gift shop. David arrives at the giftshop with James. They unlock the store and wait for the salespeople to arrive. The store manager unlocks the cash register and tells him he can leave.

David and James head home to work on some yard and house chores.

Mary comes home at 7:00 pm, harried from her day of sales at the gift shop.

"Oh my gosh, what a terrible day I had," she emotes as she comes into the kitchen where David and James are sharing a pizza. "Did you get something to eat?" she asks in a guilty tone of voice.

David holds up a piece of pizza, smiles and says, "We're good."

"I'm so sorry I'm late," Mary apologizes.

David assures her that it is no problem. He and James have been working in the yard and cleaning up the garage. Mary goes to the back of the house to change into some comfortable clothes, then emerges and starts frantically cleaning up the kitchen. David goes to the living room and turns on Monday Night Football. James goes to his room to play video games.

Mary finds a piece of pizza and goes and sits down with David. She asks, "So, how did your day go? What did you and James do? How was he?"

David looks at her with a little frustration and says, "I'm watching the game, can we discuss this later?'

Mary sits and eats her pizza and continues to try to strike up a conversation. David acts tolerant, but it's clear he is more interested in the game than what she has to say.

David just ignores her because he knows that eventually she will stop talking.

Frustrated with her husband, Mary goes back to the bedroom and calls her sister. "Hi Lucy, how's it going?"

"Fine, how are you?" she asks in a distracted tone of voice. "I only have a minute to talk."

"I just need to talk to someone, and you know it's Monday Night Football," Mary says in a dejected tone.

"Well, he's always going to watch Monday Night Football. You might as well get used to it."

"I know Lucy, but he's my husband, I just want him to acknowledge that I had a tough day at work."

"Yes, but that's probably just not going to happen on a Monday night," Lucy counseled. "He may be tired too, and that's how he unwinds. He's been with James all day, which takes a lot of energy."

"That does take a lot of energy, but it's not constant like what I deal with at the shop. And James doesn't ever complain about anything. He is very kind and sweet, and parts of the day, David gets a break," Mary says.

"Mary, I think you have unrealistic expectations for Monday Night Football. Have you talked to David about it?"

"No, he would just say I am complaining. You know David, he doesn't say much. He only talks when absolutely necessary."

"Yes, he is reserved and focused. Not everyone needs to emote the way you do," Lucy says.

Mary can feel tears welling in her eyes, but she doesn't want Lucy to know she is crying. Mary thinks about what Lucy is saying about Monday not being a good day to expect conversation from her husband. She doesn't like it very much. She decides to shift focus. "So, how was your day, Lucy?"

"Very busy. We have a bunch of new clients at work. My brain is fried."

"You sound distracted, like you need to get off the phone."

"Yes Mary, I just don't have the energy to deal with your frustration with David right now. I'm had a *really* long and tiring day too. I don't even have a husband to talk to."

"Okay, sorry you had a bad day," Mary says.

"It wasn't a bad day, just typical in the consulting world. I'll talk to you later," Lucy says. "Good-bye."

"Good-bye," Mary says and ends the call.

Mary cries silently. Now, she feels like nobody who *should* care about her does. She has spent many years feeling bad about being a bother to her husband because he doesn't talk much. And yet, she feels like there is nothing wrong with her need to relate to people verbally. She thinks about her day at the store and some of the demanding and unreasonable customers. She remembers trying to explain her return policy to one customer who was belligerent to her and said he didn't have time to hear her long explanation and numerous apologies. He just wanted his money back instantly!

"I don't deserve this," Mary thinks to herself.

She continues to anguish over her sister Lucy. "She is so full her work and her important consultant job that she doesn't even try to care about customers being rude to me.

Feeling defeated, she drifts off to sleep.

Scenario Questions

Think about the slide switch and where Mary, David and Lucy *fall* on the switch, then answer the questions below for each character in the scenario.

The Relationship Slide Switch

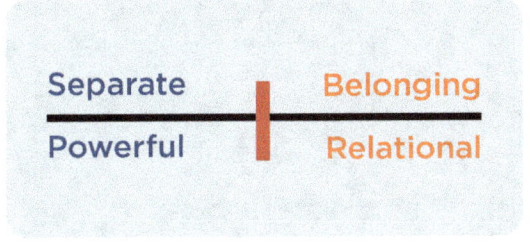

Name	Location on Slide Switch
David	
Mary	
Lucy	

Questions about David

- Based on where you think David is on the slide switch, answer the questions below if they apply.

Separate/Powerful	Belonging/Relational
What principle about belonging and relating to people is he ignoring?	What principle about results or maintaining boundaries is he ignoring?
Is he caring for and about others?	Is he doing what is right, standing on good values?
Is he considering the power of gentleness?	Is he relating without violating his values?
Is he using the truth with mercy?	Is he using truth for boundaries?
Are they pursuing the other person's best?	

- What could David do for a better outcome in his relationship with Mary?

Questions about Mary

- Based on where you think Mary is on the slide switch, answer the questions below if they apply. Answer for her relationship with David and with Lucy.

Separate/Powerful	Belonging/Relational
What principle about belonging and relating to people is she ignoring?	What principle about results or maintaining boundaries is she ignoring?
Is she caring for and about others?	Is she doing what is right, standing on good values?
Is she considering the power of gentleness?	Is she relating without violating his values?
Is she using the truth with mercy?	Is she using truth for boundaries?
Is she pursuing their best?	

- What could Mary do for a better outcome in his relationship with David?
- What could Mary do for a better outcome with her relationship with Lucy?

Questions about Lucy

- Based on where you think Lucy is on the slide switch, answer the questions below if they apply.

Separate/Powerful	Belonging/Relational
What principle about belonging and relating to people is she ignoring?	What principle about results or maintaining boundaries is she ignoring?
Is she caring for and about others?	Is she doing what is right, standing on good values?
Is she considering the power of gentleness?	Is she relating without violating his values?
Is she using the truth with mercy?	Is she using truth for boundaries?
Is she pursuing their best?	

- What could Lucy do to improve her relationship with Mary?

Are You Reflecting or Distorting God's Image?

Now that you are learning how you can reflect or distort God's image, you can begin to be aware of this critical teaching as you journey through life. Stopping and thinking about God's Image and translating it into the way to interact with people can make a big difference in relationships no matter what type they are.

Are you reflecting or distorting God's image at work? Are you using the right proportion in the way you interact with people, meaning you reflect both "sides" of God's image of Powerful and Relational in the correct amounts? Always remember that proportion is the key to the use of powerful and relational on the slide switch. If you think about "balance" it will not work for many situations in life. God always uses the right proportion so look at what He did and learn from it.

If you are not using the right proportion, you may have relationships at work that are not as impactful as they could be. For example, if you are primarily powerful toward people who work on your team, you are missing some team synergy that encourages team members to buy into what they are doing. If you seldom ask for their input, you might come across more as a dictator than a team leader. On the other hand, as a team leader if you are always asking everyone else's opinion and are constantly indecisive, you are hurting the team.

Think of your family. Do you primarily tell everyone what to do, wielding your power as a father or mother to your kids and trying to control your spouse? Or are you listening to the Lord and using the right proportion with your family, drawing on the side of God's image needed for the situation?

Let's say one of your children is on a great soccer team, one that is always winning tournaments. At one tournament your child is having an "off" day on the field and is feeling really bad about his or her performance. How do you handle that in a way that you are reflecting the right proportion of the components of God's image? Would you typically just tell your son or daughter what they need to do to be successful the next time they get on a soccer field, or would you ask some questions to better understand where they are coming from and help them process their "off" day on the field?

Reflecting God's image means being flexible within relationships and situations. How much of the relational side of His image is required and how much of the powerful side required? Within that, of course, when men and women fall into their God-given design, yet displaying God's image, it doesn't mean women cannot display the power of His image and men cannot display the relational side of His image.

What an amazing opportunity you have as a human being to reflect the image of the *Great I Am*. Think about how that can impact the world!

STUDY GUIDE

Scripture Meditation

Time: 30 minutes a day

Each day read and meditate on one of the scriptures listed below or as directed by your session leader.
Follow these steps:

1. Get in a quiet place without distraction.
2. Play a praise song, and just listen to the words.
3. Ask God to reveal His heart and meaning to you as you read the scriptures.
4. Write your reflections below or in your journal.
5. Read the scriptures daily so you receive maximum revelation.

Genesis 1:27, NKJV	Genesis 2, NKJV	Genesis 1:26-27, NKJV
Psalm 121:1-2, NKJV	Gen 9:6, NKJV	Romans 8:29, NKJV
I Corinthians 11:7, NKJV	2 Corinthians 3:18, NKJV	1 Cor 15:49, NKJV
2 Timothy 1:7, NKJV	Micah 6:8, NKJV	Isaiah 57:15, NKJV

REFLECTIVE QUESTIONS

- Why is understanding that we are made in God's image so important for understanding the design of men and women?

_____

_____

_____

_____

- How does being designed in God's image impact the fundamental design of men and women?

_____

_____

_____

_____

- Next time you have access to a hymnal, listen to Christian music, or sing in church, see if you can identify if one or both elements of God's image in a song.

_____

_____

_____

_____

- In the list below, circle the words that best describe your personality.

Separate/Powerful	Belonging/Relational
Productive	Distracter
Conspirator	Peacemaker
Blamer	Placater
Confrontational	Perceiver
Thinker	Feeler
Intuitive	Senser
Lion	Golden Retriever
Intimidating	Relational
Domineering	Compliant
Introvert	Extrovert
Beaver	Otter
Independent	Dependent
Judger	Encourager

Each list includes 13 words. Count how many words you circled in each column and record in the space provided. If you circled more words in the Separate/Powerful list, that indicates your personality tendency. If you circled more words in the Belonging/Relational list that indicates your personality tendency.

Consider your God-given design as a Man or Woman. How well does your design connect with the words you circled?

Spend some time reflecting on any disconnects you see between your behavior and design. Ask the Lord to show you any changes you need to make and how to do that.

What changes has the Lord suggested to you?

TOOLS

Each book in this series has a supplemental video course on www.tgr8relate.com/video-courses/ under the heading "BOOK SERIES Video Courses." The videos were selected from the COMPLETE Video Courses to support the book and provide more details. If you want more details than the book offers, use the COMPLETE Video Courses and the GR8 Relationships Study Guide.

The following tools will enable you to understand yourself and your spouse and how you can work together to handle conflict. The videos listed below are a part of the video course that corresponds to the information in this book. Completing all the courses will be instrumental in helping you find FREEDOM!

You can find all these tools and many more on our website, www.gr8relate.com, on the TOOLS tab.

Kolbe Assessment *https://gr8relate.com/kolbe*

You can trust the validity and accuracy of the Kolbe instrument to show you your strengths and instincts. The Kolbe also helps you easily see and understand how the strengths and talents of one person may not be considered as strengths by another. This critical information will help you bridge the gap between reality and your expectations of them. Once you complete the assessment, you will receive detailed reports that will help you understand your strengths and talents and how to use your strengths in a complementary way with your spouse, family member, or friend's strengths. By understanding your instincts, you can more easily discuss your differences, laugh about them and develop ways to deal with them.

The Thomas-Kilman Conflict Mode Instrument (TKI) https://gr8relate.com/tki

The TKI is the world's best-selling instrument for understanding conflict. It helps you see that conflict can be beneficial and useful instead of thinking conflict as bad. You will be provided detailed information on effectively using all five conflict modes—competing, collaborating, compromising, avoiding, and accommodating.

The Fundamental Interpersonal Relations Orientation-Behavior™ (FIRO-B®). https://gr8relate.com/firob

The FIRO-B helps you understand how you interact at work and personal life. This easy-to-complete assessment will provide critical insights into how an individual interacts with others. This personality instrument measures how you typically behave with others and how you expect them to act toward you.

Individual Videos

We have a FREE video course that corresponds with the information in this book._

These are short courses that you can watch/listen at your own pace. Enter the information in parenthesis below into your browser, and you will be taken to a video course. When you are online, scroll down and click the "Sign Up / Start Course" button to create an account. You only need an account to access all the free courses.

There are two options:

- BOOK SERIES Courses: Each book in the GR8 Relationships series will have a video course with specific videos selected from the COMPLETE Courses that help explain the contents of the book. This book's video course is below
  - *Made in God's Image – REALLY?* (https://gr8relate. com/video-courses/made-in- gods-image-really/)
  - COMPLETE Courses: These are the original, complete

courses that give you more details about the information in this book

- 02A – God's Design for Excellent Relationships (https://gr8relate.com/video-courses/god-design-for-excellent-relationships/)
- 02B - The Foundation of Our Design (https://gr8relate.com/video-courses/foundation-of-our-design/)
- 02C – Reflecting and Distorting God's Image (https://gr8relate.com/video-courses/reflecting-and-distorting-gods-image/)

Two Ways to Live

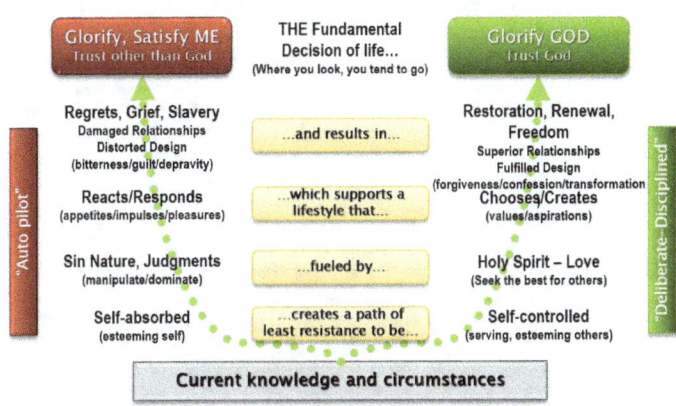

THE Fundamental Decision of life...
(Where you look, you tend to go)

Glorify, Satisfy ME
Trust other than God

Glorify GOD
Trust God

"Auto pilot"

"Deliberate – Disciplined"

Regrets, Grief, Slavery **Damaged Relationships** **Distorted Design** (bitterness/guilt/depravity)	...and results in...	Restoration, Renewal, Freedom **Superior Relationships** **Fulfilled Design** (forgiveness/confession/transformation)
Reacts/Responds (appetites/impulses/pleasures)	...which supports a lifestyle that...	Chooses/Creates (values/aspirations)
Sin Nature, Judgments (manipulate/dominate)	...fueled by...	Holy Spirit – Love (Seek the best for others)
Self-absorbed (esteeming self)	...creates a path of least resistance to be...	Self-controlled (serving, esteeming others)

Current knowledge and circumstances

You are designed in the image of God. You only need to depend upon God to allow your design to reflect the image of God. The natural tendency, though, is to depend upon yourself, which will hide or distort your design. It is automatic (AUTO PILOT) to depend on and trust YOURSELF, which follows the Self-absorbed and Judgment path. It requires a DELIBERATE choice to trust God.

When you look at your current reality, some things are known, and others aren't. Part of your current reality is you either know what God is asking you to do in this current circumstance or you don't. You either know God's Word, or you don't. God's Word is all about REALITY and how things work. If you did an objective report on your life right now, that would be a reasonable picture of your **"Current knowledge and circumstances"** or as you have learned – it is your current reality. That is where you are standing right now, in that current knowledge and circumstances rectangle.

As you stand in that rectangle, you have two clear choices or places to look. Do you remember, "Where you look, you tend to go?" God asks you where you are looking when He asks "The Fundamental Question," which is, "Do you trust God or something other than God?" That is the Fundamental Decision in life. God continually asks you that one question. It comes in two critical forms, one for our eternal life ("Do you trust Me for your eternity?") and one for our daily life ("Do you trust Me now?"). If you have accepted God's gift of Salvation, eternal life with Him, you will now be asked the second question. If you haven't you will get the first question and often the second question to drive you back to the first one. We all face these two questions. If you are blind to them, then you absolutely are depending on yourself, not God. Looking at God and trusting Him provides the best results.

If you look at **"Satisfy ME"** or "Trust something other than God," that creates a path of least resistance to being self-absorbed and self-dependent. That is the natural tendency of the sin nature to esteem yourself rather than others. When temptation comes, there is a greater chance to sin because of your self-absorbed, satisfy ME attitude. You will be less than willing to endure short-term pain, therefore

Ten Steps to Your Best Relationships!

Do you desire to have better, healthier relationships? Do you find that on some days, it seems like a struggle? If so, you are not alone. Here are ten steps that can lead you to experience your best relationships ever.

Step 1. Study God's Design for Excellent Relationships

The design of a butter knife lets you know that it works best when spreading soft things like room-temperature butter. If you try to use it to cut a T-bone steak, you will see that it is not designed to do that. The same is true for excellent relationships.

God had a clear purpose and design when He created man and woman. He designed man to be different from a woman so that the two would not only be complimentary but, more importantly, display His image to a lost and dying world.

Step 2. Recognize How Men and Women Are Different - REALLY!

God created man and woman perfectly to fulfill their designed roles which complement each other.

If you remember, God created Eve because He did not want Adam alone. Without a woman, man has no one to help "fill the earth and subdue it" (Gen 1:28). Adam needed a suitable helper to fulfill God's purpose for mankind. And for a woman, it is imperative to remember that Helper is a word used primarily about God (i.e., Ps 121:1-2), further elevating rather than demeaning women.

God designed a woman to fulfill a relational role while a man fulfills his work role design – the differences are complementary, not conflicting.

Step 3. Accept the ONE PROBLEM!

Did you know that there is only ONE PROBLEM?

Making everything about ME is THE PROBLEM that destroys relationships. It is the root from which relationship mistakes grow. Unfortunately, we are blind to how often we make life about ME! You may have noticed how easy it is to see when others are being selfish and self-absorbed, but not when you are doing it.

When others are making life about ME, it's like they have this big ME on their forehead. They cannot see it – because it is on their forehead above their eyes! The same is true for you; they see it!

Step 4. Discover the Unknown Judgments for Men and Women

Every woman and man that has, is, and will live is subject to the judgments issued by God. And this affects every relationship.

Understanding these judgments is like unlocking the secrets of what drives and motivates lousy relationships. Learning these profound judgments enables you to identify difficulties and issues in your relationships and see the damage they are creating for you now.

Woman

- **Designed to RELATE:** The woman's unique design helps, nurtures, and supports healthy relationships, especially with her husband and children.
- **RELATING is Judged:** The woman's judgment adds pain to relationships and drives her to control them, which creates more pain, especially with her husband and children.

51 Relationship Principles

1. Think of others as important, in fact, more important than you.

2. 3 Simple Guidelines; 3 Simple Questions
   a. Do what is right. Will I do what is right?
   b. Be trustworthy. Will I commit to doing my best?
   c. Do to others as you would have them do to you. Will I pursue the good of and serve others more than myself?

3. Freedom in relationships does not mean license; it primarily involves being a real person and letting others be themselves.

4. Freedom blossoms relationships: control and manipulation limit them.

5. Freedom in marriage allows each person to operate in their design.

6. If people are not free to be themselves around you, then, most likely, your relationships are all about YOU.

7. When freedom and choice are not in a relationship, someone is being controlled (dominated or manipulated).

8. When you cannot be yourself in a relationship, the relationship will become intolerable.

9. When freedom and choice are in a relationship, the whole person (good & bad) is accepted.

10. When you are tense, angry, frustrated, or irritated, it often means someone is not doing the job you assigned them.

11. Your happiness is a lousy job to assign to anyone or anything. Why let someone else control you that way?

12. When you take things personally, you are not operating in freedom.

13. Without freedom in a relationship, someone will be a fake, hypocrite, or liar.

14. If a relationship must satisfy you, you are walking down the manipulation trail (You are saying NO to the relationship and making the relationship about you; freedom is limited).

15. Relationships happen in reality, in real-time, with real people.

16. No one owes you anything in a relationship.

17. The closer you are to change, the greater will be the resistance.

18. To the degree we deny our issues, we will find a scapegoat on which to dump them.

19. Victims are focused on getting their circumstances and those around them to change, not on changing themselves.

20. Victims must be rescued; they are dependent on circumstances or others' changes to make them happy.

21. Draw a line in the sand and create a new past.

22. Give people more than they expect cheerfully.

242 Spring Park Drive, Ste A   Midland, Texas 79705   Phone: 432-682-6823   https://gr8relate.com   Email: info.gr8relate@gr8grp.com

Pursuing Their BEST
– In Work, In Life, In Love

Conflict RESOLVED BluePrint

Remember 4+3+2 Essentials

4 Critical Principles	3 Cardinal Rules	2 Skills	5 Styles
·RELATIONSHIPS: WE, not just ME ·FUTURE: The Past is OVER ·FREEDOM: Don't try to change them ·KINDNESS: Kindness instead of winning	·SLOW the emotions down ·TALK until a solution is found ·Seek TWO-sided solutions	·Listening ·Asking Questions	·Accommodating ·Avoiding ·Collaborating ·Competing ·Compromising

Evaluate the Conflict: Questions...

Conflict	You	Them	Meeting
·What is it about? ·What are the components? ·How will it impact the relationship? ·Will we 1) battle until the other changes? 2) disagree and end relationship, 3) disagree and keep relationship 4) resolve and keep relationship 5) resolve and end the relationship	·What was my role, contribution? ·What resolution do I want? ·What are my needs, goals? ·Do I need them? ·Are my expectations reasonable? ·What misperceptions might they have of me?	·Am I defining them by their negative behavior? ·What are their needs? ·Do I understand their side? ·What misperceptions might I have of them? ·What buttons do they have?	·What Method? ·What Time? ·What Location?

Set the Ground Rules

3 Cardinal Rules	General Rules		Good Values
·SLOW the emotions down ·TALK until solution is found ·Seek TWO-sided solutions	·Be Clear ·"Speak to the center of the room" ·No attacking or blaming ·One person speaks at a time	·Look at each other when speaking ·All ideas as valid when presented ·Build on each other's ideas ·Explore each idea	·Be Fair ·Be Honest ·Be Responsible ·Be Respectful ·Be Considerate

Open the Conversation

Open and honest about seeking a solution	Partner with them; create a WE atmosphere	Encourage options through shared effort	Narrow the scope – agreement on everything is not required

Listen and Clarify

Focus only on them	Observe what they say	Seek facts with good questions	Summarize; check what you heard	Summarize often	Seek Permission

Value and Seek Options

Criteria for Good Options	Meets one or more shared needs	Meets one or more needs not incompatible with other party	Potential to improve future relationship	Can be supported by all parties
Uncover Options	Seek their options first	Learn from the past	Keep your ears open!	

Establish A Solution

·WE (2-sided solutions) ·Thinking (Slow emotions down) ·Facts (talk)	·Focus on shared needs ·Increase the size of the pie	Behavior specific	Document it

Decide to Follow-up

Love, True Love!

What is true love?

Do a Google search on "What is Love." From a world's perspective, here are some things you will find:

- Love is an emotion that keeps people bonded and committed to one another.
- Love is about give and take.
- Love is an intense deep affection for another person.

Then there is the dictionary definition. Webster defines love as:

- A strong affection for one another
- Attraction based on sexual desire
- Affection based on admiration
- Warm attachment or devotion
- Unselfish loyal & benevolent concern for the good of another
- An amorous episode between two people
- A sexual embrace

Do you notice that most of these definitions don't say anything about the one loved? The World completely misses the beauty of love as God has described it.

World's "love" is selfish.

The World's love encourages the "flashing ME," making life about yourself. You seek your good above the good of others. The World's view of love too often wants to control others.

World's "love" is conditional.

The World's love depends upon your needs being met, and you will "love" them as long as that happens. No longer is it okay to have them say they love you; it requires proof!

World's "love" is temporary.

When you are unhappy, when things get uncomfortable or difficult in the relationship, or when you no longer feel loved or loving, love is gone. That "love" is as fleeting as magic fairy dust that gets blown away in high wind. It knows nothing of patience.

What about "falling in love?" When you fall, it is not something you decide to do; it happens to you, right? You are caught in a wave of feelings, sprinkled with love dust, and poof, you are now in love!

Yes, I do believe in "chemistry" between people. It is real, but that is attraction, not love. If you can "fall in love," you can "fall out of love." When the love dust is gone, you no longer love them. In other words, that view says love is some force of the universe that stays with you or doesn't, entirely out of your control.

ENDNOTES

1   Roy Zuck, Biblical Theology of the Old Testament, pages 12-14

2   Ibid.

3   John Calvin, translation of Henry Beveridge, Esq., Institutes of Christian Religion, 1581s

4   The Teacher's Commentary, (Wheaton, IL: Victor Books) 1987.

5   Walvoord, John F., and Zuck, Roy B., The Bible Knowledge Commentary, (Wheaton, Illinois: Scripture Press Publications, Inc.) 1983, 1985

6   The New Bible Dictionary, (Wheaton, Illinois: Tyndale House Publishers, Inc.) 1962.